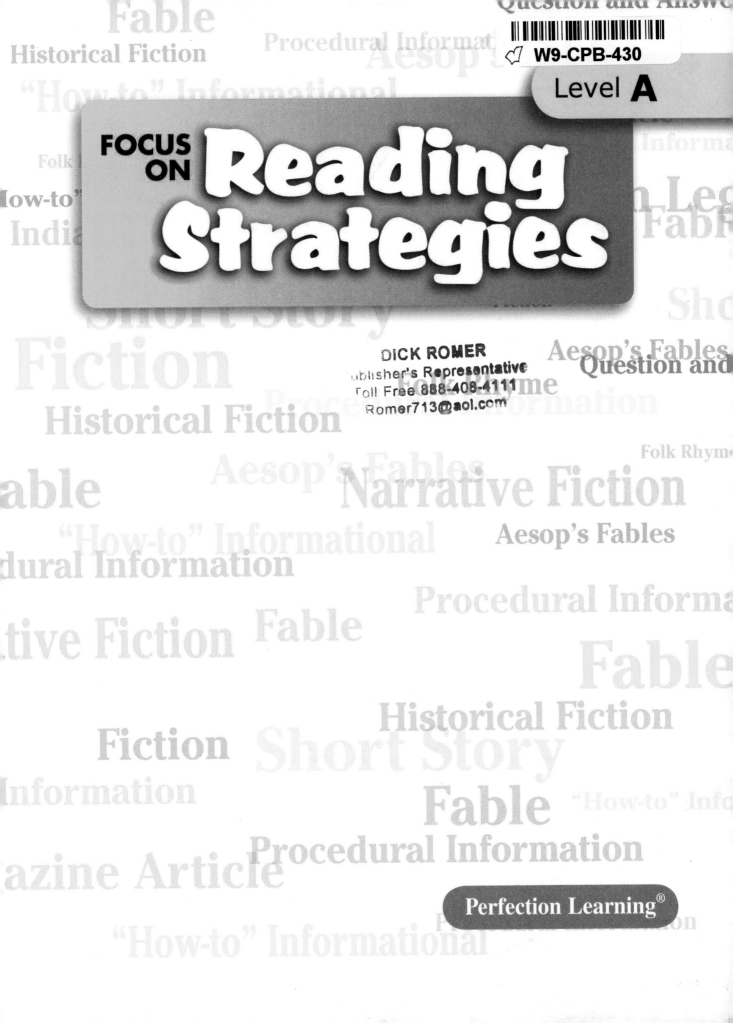

Level **A**

FOCUS ON Reading Strategies

Perfection Learning®

Editorial Director: Susan C. Thies
Editor: Kathryn Winzenburg
Design Director: Randy Messer
Cover Design: Michael A. Aspengren
Book Design: Deborah Lea Bell
Contributing Designers: Michael A. Aspengren, Michelle Glass, Emily Greazel

Reviewers:

Kathryn Black
Language Program Specialist
Mesa Public Schools
Mesa, Arizona

Cindy Brunswick
Literacy Coordinator
Center for School Improvement
University of Chicago
Chicago, Illinois

L. Michelle Johnson, M.Ed.
Education Department
Washington College
Chestertown, Maryland

Jan Keese
K–12 Reading Facilitator
Ankeny Community Schools
Ankeny, Iowa

Photo Credits: ©Corbis pp. 27 (bottom), 28 (bottom); ©Kent Vilet p. 82 (inset)

Some images www.clipart.com; www.photos.com; Corel Professional Photos; Dynamic Graphics Liquid Library; istockphoto.com; ©Perfection Learning Corporation

Illustration Credits: Michael A. Aspengren pp. 20, 28, 30, 51, 52; Sue F. Cornelison pp. 32, 72; Doug Keith pp. 34, 36; Dea Marks pp. 68, 70; Randy Messer pp. 6, 8, 11

For information, contact
Perfection Learning® Corporation
1000 North Second Avenue, P.O. Box 500
Logan, Iowa 51546-0500
Phone: 1-800-831-4190
Fax: 1-800-543-2745
perfectionlearning.com

ISBN 0-7891-6790-5

1 2 3 4 5 6 BA 11 10 09 08 07 06

Table of Contents

continued

Section 2

Lesson 1

from
Great Eagle
and Small One

Heads Up Look at the picture. Read the sentence. Then answer the question.

Great Eagle hunted.

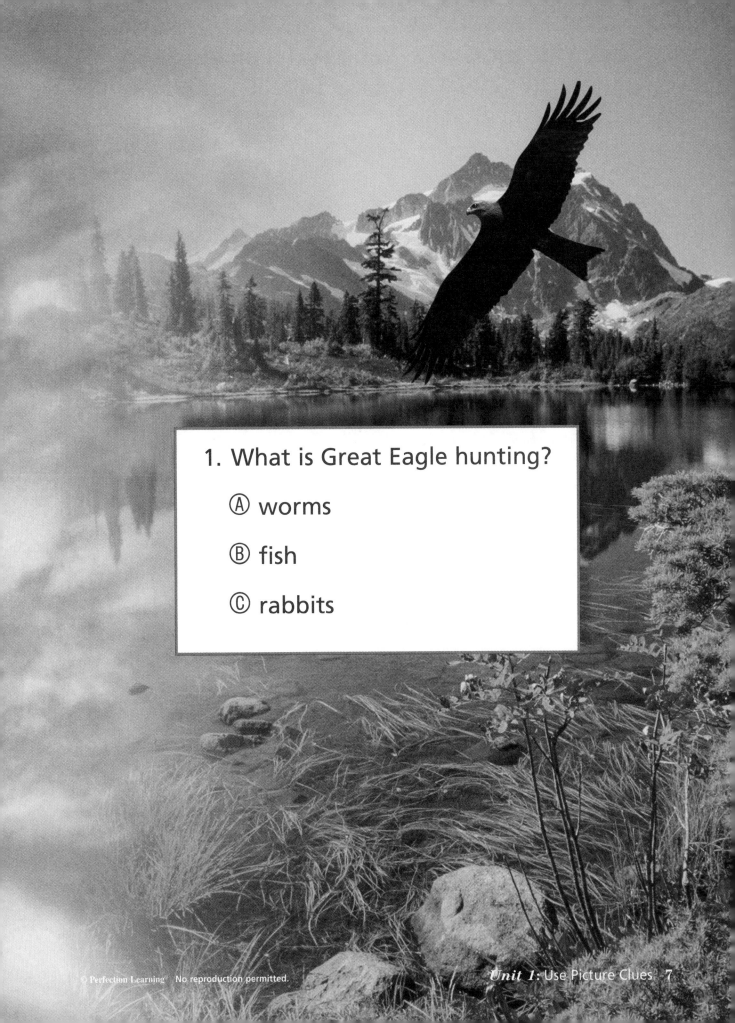

1. What is Great Eagle hunting?

Ⓐ worms

Ⓑ fish

Ⓒ rabbits

Read the sentences. Look at the picture.

After many tries, Great Eagle stood. But he did not stand straight like before. His body was bent.

Make Sense of Words Use the picture clues. Answer the questions.

1. Why can't Great Eagle stand straight?

    Ⓐ His wing is broken.

    Ⓑ He is old.

    Ⓒ He has lost his left foot.

2. What word means the opposite of *straight*?

    Ⓐ bent

    Ⓑ tries

    Ⓒ stood

3. What part of Great Eagle's body is bent?

    Ⓐ his leg

    Ⓑ his wing

    Ⓒ his head

1. What can you tell about Great Eagle?

   Ⓐ He is trying to fly.

   Ⓑ He can balance on one foot.

   Ⓒ He has a broken wing.

Understand by Seeing It

Use the picture clues. Choose the sentence in each pair that fits. Write the letter in one of the circles.

a. Great Eagle's legs are bent.

b. Great Eagle's head is bent.

c. Great Eagle's left foot is missing.

d. Great Eagle's right foot is missing.

e. Great Eagle can stand.

f. Great Eagle can't stand.

Great Eagle

Write to Learn Draw a picture to match the sentence below.

Great Eagle flew.

Lesson 2

Building a Birdhouse

Heads Up Look at the picture. Read the directions. Then answer the question.

Glue the four walls together.

1. This picture helps by showing

   Ⓐ all four walls glued together.

   Ⓑ how to glue the fourth wall on.

   Ⓒ where the roof goes.

Make Sense of Words Look at the picture.
Read the sentences. Answer the questions.

Find the bottom of the birdhouse.

Glue the bottom onto the house.

1. What is meant by *the bottom* of the birdhouse?

   Ⓐ the floor

   Ⓑ the roof

   Ⓒ the grass

2. Which of the directions is the girl following?

   Ⓐ Find the bottom of the birdhouse.

   Ⓑ Glue the roof to the top.

   Ⓒ Glue the bottom onto the house.

3. What part of the birdhouse will come next?

   Ⓐ the walls

   Ⓑ the roof

   Ⓒ the perch

1. What can you tell about the birdhouse from the picture?

    Ⓐ It is made of metal.

    Ⓑ It is very large.

    Ⓒ It is made of wood.

Choose the direction sentence to match each picture.
Write it on the blank below the picture.

Glue the roof pieces together.
Glue the bottom onto the house.

_____   _____

_____   _____

Put glue on the first wall.

Paint the birdhouse.

Glue the roof onto the house.

_____

_____

_____

_____

_____

Write to Learn Add one more direction.
Then draw a picture to match.

_____

from Wheels!

Heads Up Read the sentences. Then answer the question.

Imagine a wagon race. Both wagons are the same size. They carry the same load. But one wagon has wheels. The other is like a sled. It has runners.

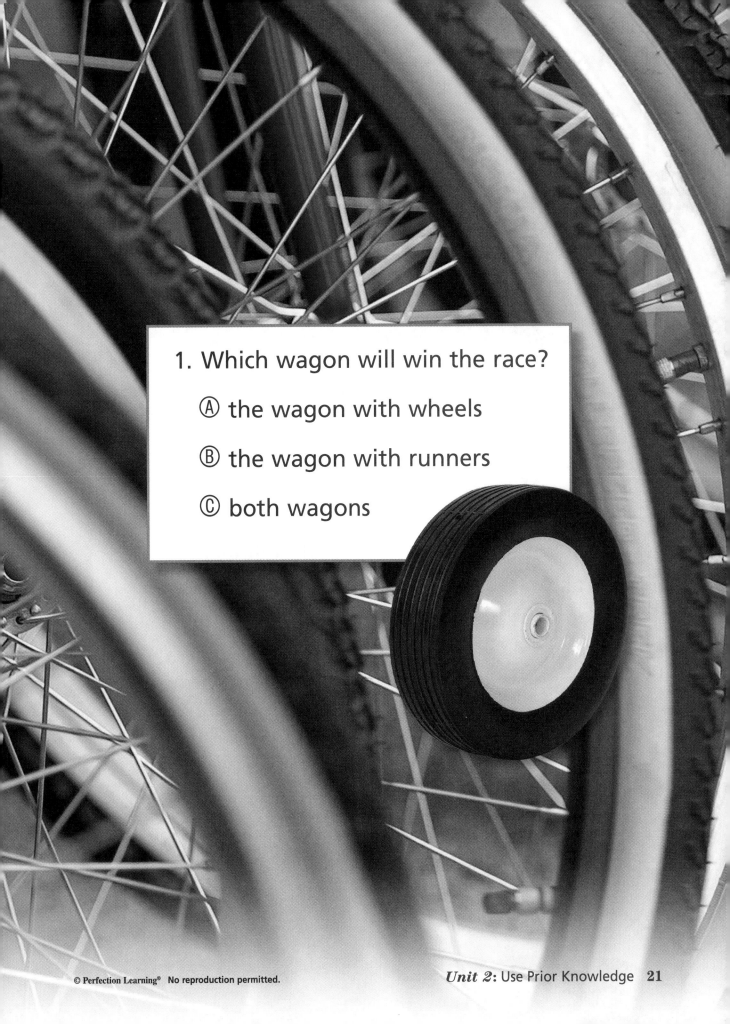

1. Which wagon will win the race?

Ⓐ the wagon with wheels

Ⓑ the wagon with runners

Ⓒ both wagons

Read the sentences. Then answer the questions.

Skateboards were invented after roller skates. They are like little surfboards on roller skate wheels. The wheels are fastened to the bottom of the narrow board. Kids ride them like scooters.

Make Sense of Words Use what you already know to answer the questions.

1. What are roller skates?

    Ⓐ a board with wheels on the bottom

    Ⓑ shoes with runners on the bottom

    Ⓒ shoes with wheels on the bottom

2. What word means the opposite of *bottom*?

    Ⓐ under

    Ⓑ top

    Ⓒ below

3. Where would you use a surfboard?

    Ⓐ in the water

    Ⓑ on the street

    Ⓒ in the air

1. How is a scooter like a skateboard?

   Ⓐ Both have handlebars.

   Ⓑ Both are used in the water.

   Ⓒ Both have wheels.

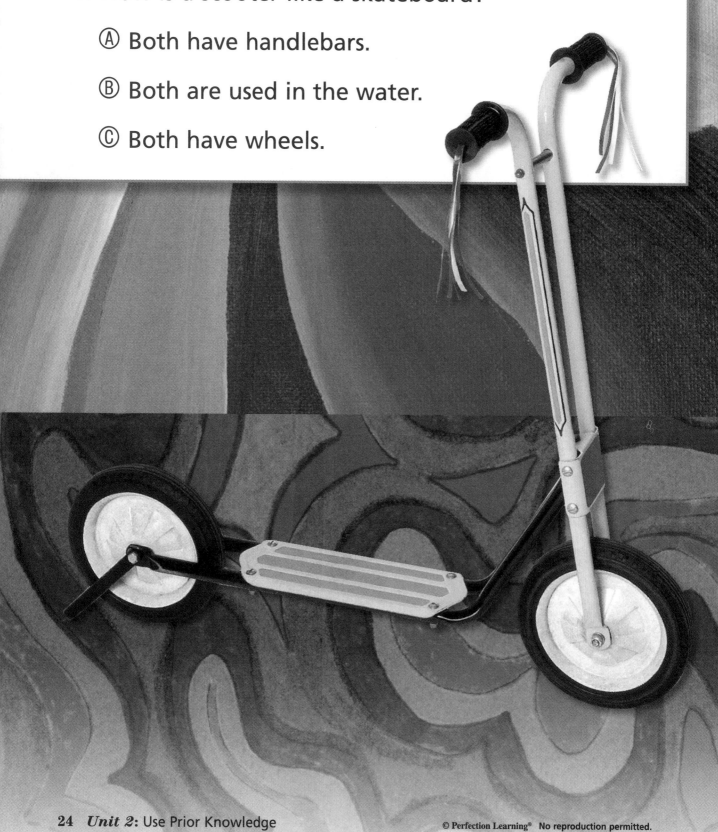

Understand by Seeing It Use what you know about wheels. Choose four things in the list that have wheels. Write each one in a circle.

car   book   bike   telephone

bus   train   dog   sled

Things with **wheels**

Write to Learn Draw a picture of something you use that has wheels. Then write a sentence describing it.

_____

Lesson 4

from

The Four Seasons

Heads Up Read the sentences. Then answer the question.

It is a cool day at the park. Families ride bikes on the path. The leaves are yellow, red, and orange. Kids zip up their sweatshirts as they feed bread crumbs to the ducks.

1. What season is it?

Ⓐ winter

Ⓑ summer

Ⓒ fall

Read the sentences. Then answer the questions.

It is a cold day at the park. The trees have no leaves. Snowflakes fall. The pond is frozen. The ducks have flown south. Kids wear hats, scarves, and warm coats. Sleds dot the hillside.

Make Sense of Words Use what you already know to answer the questions.

1. What is another word for *pond*?

   Ⓐ lake

   Ⓑ grass

   Ⓒ sky

2. What are snowflakes made of?

   Ⓐ leaves

   Ⓑ snow

   Ⓒ paper

3. What are scarves?

   Ⓐ things you wear

   Ⓑ things you eat

   Ⓒ things you plant

Read with Understanding Use the sentences on page 28 and what you already know. Answer the question.

1. What season is it?

   Ⓐ winter

   Ⓑ spring

   Ⓒ summer

Understand by Seeing It The four seasons occur in the same order every year. Use what you already know to put "spring" and "fall" on the season timeline.

Winter

_____

Summer

_____

Write to Learn Draw a picture of your favorite season. Then write a sentence explaining why it is your favorite.

_____

Lesson 5

from

Brit Knits *and* Pat at Bat

Heads Up Read the sentences. Then answer the question.

Little Brit gets her kit. She goes to sit near a candle lit. Brit admits she loves to knit. She sticks with it and doesn't quit. She makes a slit for the button to fit. And, bit by bit, it's a new outfit.

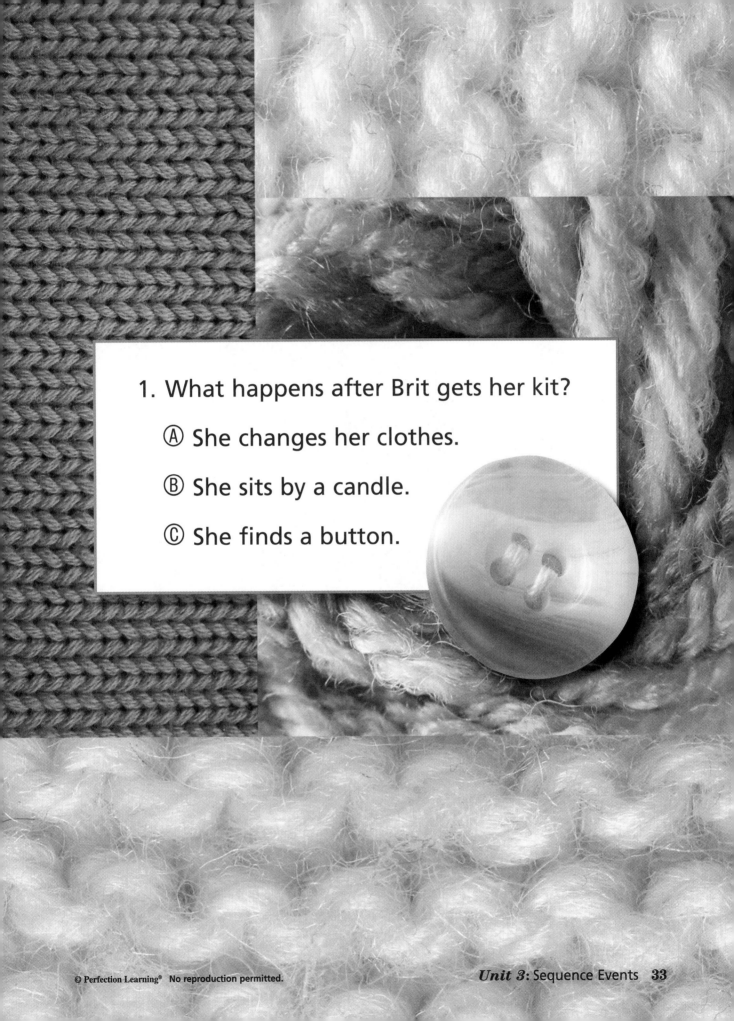

1. What happens after Brit gets her kit?

Ⓐ She changes her clothes.

Ⓑ She sits by a candle.

Ⓒ She finds a button.

Pat, the cat, is up at bat. He pulls his hat and taps the mat. But then, a rat shouts out, "Drat!"

"Can you believe that? My soda's flat!"

1. What word means the opposite of *shouts*?

   Ⓐ whispers

   Ⓑ screams

   Ⓒ yells

2. What is another word for *soda*?

   Ⓐ sugar

   Ⓑ food

   Ⓒ pop

3. What does Pat tap in the story?

   Ⓐ the hat

   Ⓑ the mat

   Ⓒ the rat

Read with Understanding Use the order of events in the sentences on page 34 to answer the question.

1. What happens before Pat taps the mat?

   Ⓐ Pat pulls on his hat.

   Ⓑ The rat yells, "Drat!"

   Ⓒ The rat's soda is flat.

Understand by Seeing It These events are from the story. Put them in order from first to last. Write each sentence in the correct box.

Pat pulls his hat.
A rat yells, "Drat!"
Pat goes up to bat.
Pat taps the mat.

1. _____

2. _____

3. _____

4. _____

Lesson 6

from
Saturday Night PIZZA

Heads Up Read the sentences. Then answer the question.

Every Saturday night, we get to order pizza for supper. Then we eat together and watch movies.

1. When does the family eat?

Ⓐ before they order pizza

Ⓑ while they watch movies

Ⓒ after they watch movies

Dad uses his cell phone to call in the order. The order will be ready in 10 minutes, so Dad leaves right away. He drives to the pizza shop. Dad arrives just in time. The pizza is just coming out of the oven as Dad walks in.

1. What does the oven do?

    Ⓐ bakes the pizza

    Ⓑ shapes the pizza

    Ⓒ eats the pizza

2. How does the dad get to the pizza shop?

    Ⓐ He walks.

    Ⓑ He rides a bike.

    Ⓒ He drives.

3. What word means the opposite of *arrives*?

    Ⓐ walks

    Ⓑ leaves

    Ⓒ drives

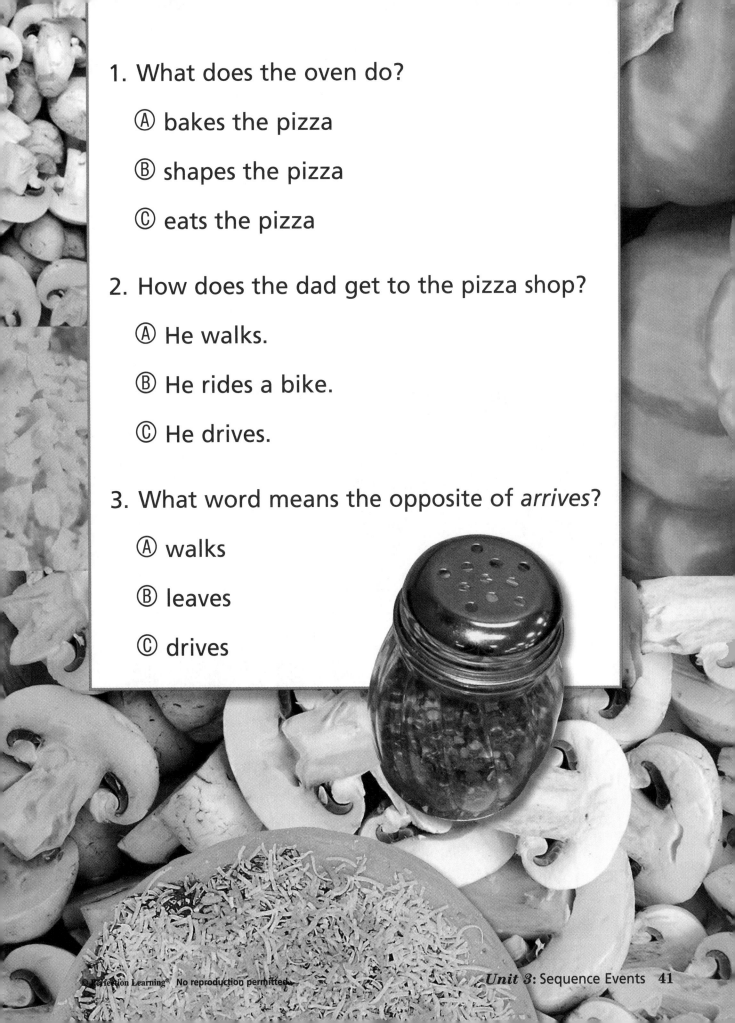

Read with Understanding Reread the sentences on page 40. Use the order of events to answer the question.

1. What does the dad do right after he calls in the pizza order?

   Ⓐ He leaves for the pizza shop.

   Ⓑ He walks in when the pizza is done.

   Ⓒ He uses his cell phone.

Understand by Seeing It The pictures below are from the passage. Put them in order by numbering them with a *1*, *2*, and *3*.

Dad calls in the order.

☐ _____

The pizza is coming out of the oven as Dad walks in.

☐ _____

Dad drives to the pizza shop.

☐ _____

Write to Learn Cheese pizza is made with cheese, crust, and pizza sauce. Write three sentences that tell which ingredient goes first, second, and third when making a pizza.

_____

_____

_____

_____

_____

_____

_____

_____

from Which One Doesn't Belong?

Heads Up Read the sentences. Look at the pictures. Then answer the questions on the next page.

Which one doesn't belong? Is it the lizard, the polar bear, the penguin, or the fox? The lizard likes it hot.

Read with Understanding

1. What is in all of the pictures except the one with the lizard?

   Ⓐ an animal

   Ⓑ snow

   Ⓒ rocks

2. Use what you already know. Which animal doesn't belong?

   Ⓐ lizard

   Ⓑ polar bear

   Ⓒ penguin

3. Which animal is listed last on page 45?

   Ⓐ polar bear

   Ⓑ penguin

   Ⓒ fox

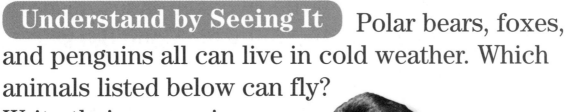

Understand by Seeing It Polar bears, foxes, and penguins all can live in cold weather. Which animals listed below can fly? Write their names in the circles.

butterfly   cow

bird   bat

Animals that can fly

Write to Learn Write two sentences describing the four animals below. Tell which one doesn't belong and why.

butterfly   bird   cow   bat

_____

_____

_____

_____

_____

_____

_____

_____

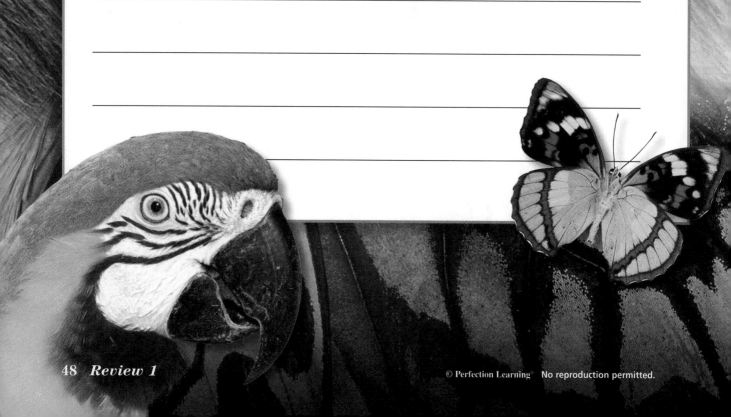

The CROW and the PITCHER

Listen as your teacher reads. Then answer the questions.

1. Why wasn't the Crow able to drink the water?

   Ⓐ His beak wasn't long enough.

   Ⓑ There were pebbles in the water.

   Ⓒ He wasn't thirsty.

2. Which of the following lessons did the Crow learn?

   Ⓐ Water is not good to drink.

   Ⓑ Keep trying. Don't give up.

   Ⓒ Friends are good to have.

Lesson 7
from The Mystery of Apartment A-13

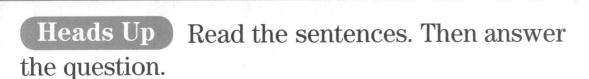

Heads Up Read the sentences. Then answer the question.

"Do you know who lives in apartment A-13?" Ty asked Gabe.

"No," said Gabe. "It's always dark at night. Maybe it's empty."

"I don't think so," said Ty. "Every day someone brings a sack. And they leave with a sack. Someone has to be in there."

"I have a great idea!" said Gabe.

1. What do you think Gabe will suggest?

   Ⓐ They should live in apartment A-13.

   Ⓑ They should play basketball.

   Ⓒ They should find out who lives in apartment A-13.

Make Sense of Words Read the sentences. Then answer the questions.

"Ty and I will listen at the door," said Gabe.

Ty and Gabe walked across the parking lot. They climbed to the third floor. They listened at the door of apartment A-13. Then they heard it! Ty and Gabe looked at each other. Their mouths dropped open. And their eyes got bigger.

1. What is a word that means the opposite of *open*?

    Ⓐ closed

    Ⓑ in

    Ⓒ down

2. What is an apartment?

    Ⓐ a store

    Ⓑ a school

    Ⓒ a home

3. What do Ty and Gabe probably hear?

    Ⓐ nothing

    Ⓑ strange noises

    Ⓒ their friends

Read with Understanding Use the sentences on page 52. Answer the question.

1. What will Ty and Gabe do next?

Ⓐ run back home

Ⓑ have a snack

Ⓒ go to school

Understand by Seeing It Knowing the main events of a story can help you make a prediction. Draw the main events listed.

1. Ty and Gabe go to spy on apartment A-13.

2. They hear something strange.

3. Their mouths drop open, and their eyes grow bigger.

Write to Learn What do you think the strange noises Ty and Gabe heard might be? Draw a picture of your prediction. Then write a sentence explaining what it is.

Lesson 8
from WHAT'S THE PROBLEM?

Heads Up Read the sentences. Then answer the question.

Many people cannot see well. They need help.

1. What invention helps people see better?

Ⓐ zippers

Ⓑ eyeglasses

Ⓒ umbrellas

Make Sense of Words Read the sentences. Then answer the questions.

Can you imagine writing books by hand? Six hundred years ago, all books were written by hand. It was hard work. There were not enough books for everyone.

1. What is another word for *hard*?

    Ⓐ soft

    Ⓑ easy

    Ⓒ tough

2. Why weren't there enough books for everyone?

    Ⓐ It was hard work writing books by hand.

    Ⓑ Six hundred years ago was a long time.

    Ⓒ No one could read.

3. What is the opposite of *all books*?

    Ⓐ many books

    Ⓑ every book

    Ⓒ no books

Read with Understanding
Use the sentences on page 58 to make a prediction.

1. What invention solved this problem?

Ⓐ lightbulb

Ⓑ printing press

Ⓒ dryer

Understand by Seeing It
Without technology, life would be much different. Choose four things from the list below that are inventions. Write each one in a circle.

| computer | dirt | skin | airplane |
| telephone | car | water | |

Inventions

Write to Learn Draw a picture of an invention you use every day. Then write a sentence describing it.

Lesson 9

from

Henry and Mudge: The First Book

Heads Up Read about Henry. Then answer the question.

> Henry used to walk to school alone. When he walked alone he used to worry about tornadoes, ghosts, biting dogs, and bullies.

1. Which word best describes Henry?

    Ⓐ brave

    Ⓑ mean

    Ⓒ worried

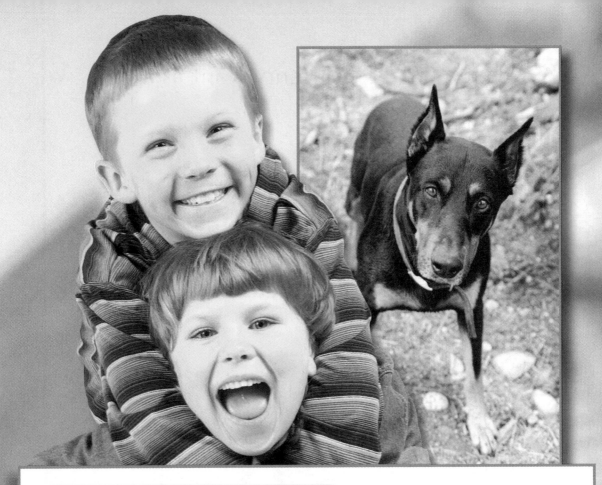

Make Sense of Words   Read the sentences.
Then answer the questions on pages 64 and 65.

Henry had no brothers and no sisters.
"I want a brother," he told his parents.

"Sorry," they said.

Henry had no friends on his street.
"I want to live on a different street," he told
his parents.

"Sorry," they said.

Henry had no pets at home.
"I want to have a dog," he told his parents.

1. What animal does Henry want as a pet?

   Ⓐ cat

   Ⓑ dog

   Ⓒ fish

2. What is a word that means the opposite of *different*?

   Ⓐ same

   Ⓑ bad

   Ⓒ new

3. How many brothers and sisters does Henry have?

   Ⓐ 0

   Ⓑ 1

   Ⓒ 2

Read with Understanding

1. What word describes Henry?

   Ⓐ mean

   Ⓑ fun

   Ⓒ lonely

Understand by Seeing It Henry asks his parents for three things. List the three things in order in the boxes below.

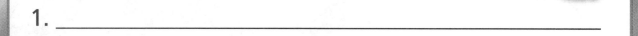

1. _____

2. _____

3. _____

Write to Learn Think of yourself as a character. Write two sentences describing yourself. Then draw a picture of yourself.

_____

_____

_____

_____

Lesson 10

from Little Fish

> **Heads Up** Read the sentences. Then answer the question.

It was time to jump into the deepest part of the river. Little Fish was scared. How would she ever jump that far? She wondered if she should try at all. It was so hard being the smallest.

Old One knew what Little Fish was thinking. He spoke to her. "Little Fish, do not worry. If you try, you will be able to follow me."

1. How would you describe Old One?

Ⓐ helpful

Ⓑ mean

Ⓒ scared

Make Sense of Words Read the sentences. Then answer the questions.

Little Fish knew what she had to do to jump over the rock. She started swimming fast and hard. Back and forth she swam. Over and over she jumped.

This went on for several days. Little Fish didn't know it, but each day she was getting stronger. She swam a little faster. And she jumped a little higher.

1. Where do fish swim?

    Ⓐ in the air

    Ⓑ on land

    Ⓒ in the water

2. What is Little Fish doing?

    Ⓐ playing

    Ⓑ practicing

    Ⓒ running

3. What does *several days* mean?

    Ⓐ many days

    Ⓑ more than one month

    Ⓒ two months

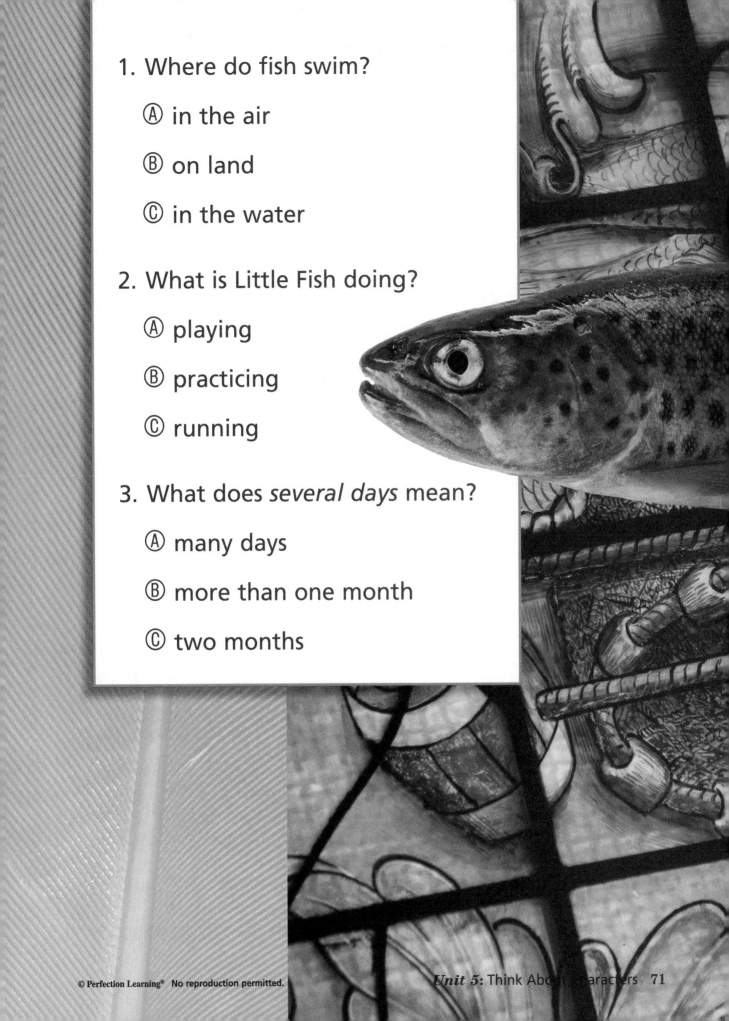

Read with Understanding Use the sentences on page 70 to answer the question.

1. Which sentence best describes Little Fish?

   Ⓐ Little Fish doesn't want to try to jump.

   Ⓑ Little Fish doesn't want to leave her home.

   Ⓒ Little Fish is determined to jump over the rock.

Understand by Seeing It You learn a lot about Little Fish in this story. Write three words that describe Little Fish below.

Write to Learn   Now that you know Little Fish, what do you think will happen to her? Will she make it over the rock? Write a sentence that tells what you think will happen to Little Fish. Draw a picture to go with it.

_____

_____

_____

Lesson 11

from Arthur Tricks the Tooth Fairy

Heads Up Read the sentences. Then answer the question.

Arthur ran to the breakfast table.
"Look, D.W.," he said. Arthur waved a dollar.
"The Tooth Fairy left it under my pillow."

"Why?" asked D.W.

"She takes baby teeth and leaves money," Arthur said.

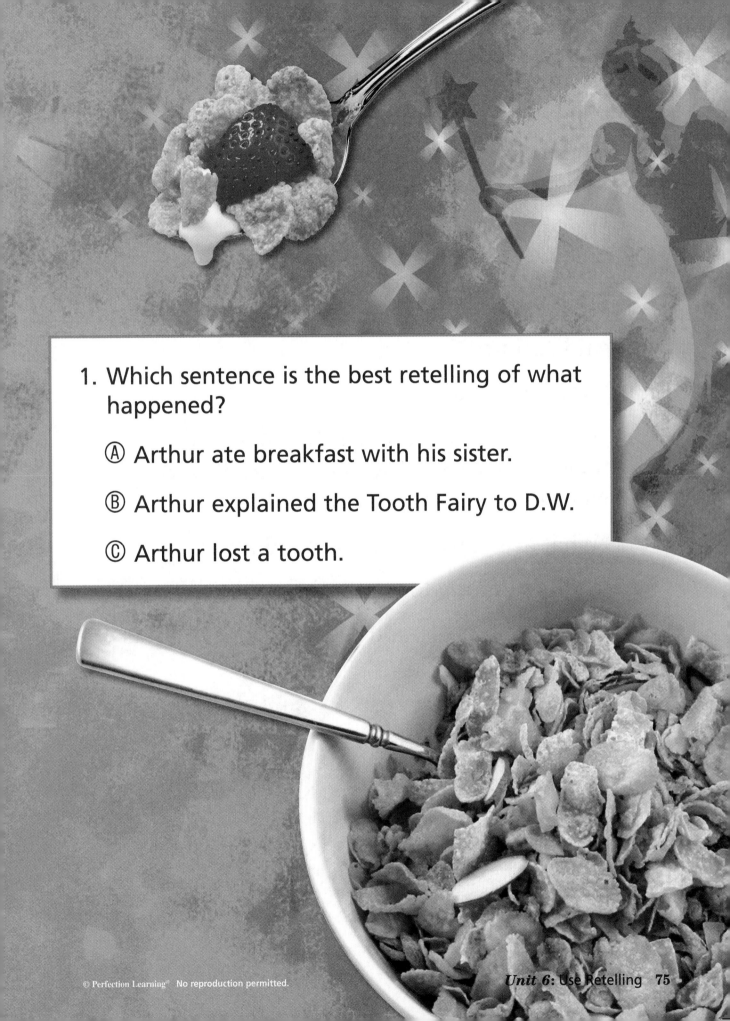

1. Which sentence is the best retelling of what happened?

Ⓐ Arthur ate breakfast with his sister.

Ⓑ Arthur explained the Tooth Fairy to D.W.

Ⓒ Arthur lost a tooth.

Read the sentences. Then answer the questions.

The next morning D.W. ran to the breakfast table. "My tooth is loose!" she shouted.

"It is not," Arthur said.

"Is too," said D.W.

"Nope. You are too young to lose teeth," said Arthur.

"Not fair!" said D.W.

When Arthur got home from school, the house was very noisy. Slam! SLAM! **SLAM!** went D.W.'s door.

"What are you doing?" shouted Arthur.

"Pulling out my loose tooth," said D.W.

"Oh, no! Stop it!" said Arthur. "Your tooth is NOT loose."

1. What does *noisy* mean?

   Ⓐ loud

   Ⓑ quiet

   Ⓒ big

2. Why can't D.W. lose a tooth?

   Ⓐ She is too old.

   Ⓑ She is too young.

   Ⓒ She doesn't have teeth.

3. Why does Arthur tell D.W. to stop?

   Ⓐ He wants her to get hurt.

   Ⓑ He doesn't like the noise.

   Ⓒ Her tooth isn't loose.

Read with Understanding Use the story. Answer the question.

1. Why does D.W. want to lose a tooth?

Ⓐ She wants to have a visit from the Tooth Fairy.

Ⓑ She likes the way it feels.

Ⓒ She thinks she has too many teeth.

Understand by Seeing It When you retell a story, you need to know what information to include. Read the sentences. Choose two that are important to include in a retelling. Write them in the boxes.

1. "Not fair!"

2. "You are too young to lose teeth," said Arthur.

3. D.W. ran to the breakfast table.

4. "Pulling out my loose tooth," said D.W.

Write to Learn   Write three sentences that retell what happened in the story. If you need to, go back and read the story again.

_____

_____

_____

_____

_____

_____

_____

Lesson 12

from

Scaly and Scary

Heads Up Read the sentences. Then answer the question.

Alligators are cold-blooded reptiles. That does not mean that they have cold blood. Their inside temperature is the same as the temperature around them. Alligators bask in the sun when they are too cold. When they are hot, they move to the shade or into the water.

1. What important fact do these sentences explain?

   Ⓐ Alligators like to bask in the sun.

   Ⓑ Alligators don't like water.

   Ⓒ Alligators are cold-blooded.

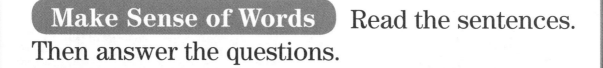

Make Sense of Words Read the sentences. Then answer the questions.

The mother alligator lays around 30 to 50 eggs. She makes a pile of leaves, grass, and dirt. Then she digs a hole in the pile for her eggs. She covers the eggs with leaves and mud. While she waits for the eggs to hatch, she digs a pool nearby. Young alligators use an egg tooth on their snout to break out of their shell. When the mother hears the babies squeak, she digs them out.

1. What is a snout?

   Ⓐ an ear   Ⓑ a nose   Ⓒ an eye

2. Which word means the opposite of *nearby*?

   Ⓐ far   Ⓑ close   Ⓒ next

3. What does the mother alligator use to build her nest?

   Ⓐ bugs   Ⓑ mud   Ⓒ fish

Read with Understanding   Reread the sentences. Answer the question.

1. How many eggs can a mother alligator lay?

   Ⓐ 10 to 20

   Ⓑ 30 to 50

   Ⓒ 70 to 90

Understand by Seeing It Think about telling someone what you learned about how alligators are born. Use the sentences below. Fill in the blanks in order.

> She waits for the eggs to hatch by digging a pool nearby.
> The mother alligator lays the eggs.
> The mother digs the baby alligators out.

1. _____

2. She makes a pile of leaves, grass, and dirt where she puts the eggs.

3. _____

4. The young alligators break out of the eggs with their egg tooth.

5. _____

Write to Learn Draw a picture of an alligator. Then write two new things that you learned about alligators from the passage.

from Junie B., First Grader (at last!)

On Monday morning, Grace got on the bus with a *new* girl from her class. And those two plopped down in the seat right in front of me!

I quick jumped up. And I tapped on Grace's head.

"Grace?" I said. "*Excuse* me. Grace? What kind of shenanigans do you call this, madam? Didn't you see me sitting here?"

Grace waved at me real friendly. "Yes. Hi, Junie B.," she said. "I'm sorry I can't sit with you today. But I promised Bobbi Jean Piper I would sit with her this morning. Okay?"

I stamped my foot. "No, Grace. *Not* okay. You can't sit with Bobbi Jean Piper," I said. "You and I have to sit together every single day. 'Cause we sat together every day last year. And this year shalt be no different."

Just then, Mr. Woo, the bus driver, closed the bus door. He looked in his mirror.

1. What do you think Mr. Woo will say to Junie B.?

   Ⓐ "Dance down the aisle."

   Ⓑ "Get off the bus."

   Ⓒ "Sit down."

2. Which word best describes Grace?

   Ⓐ friendly

   Ⓑ scared

   Ⓒ angry

3. How does Junie B. feel about Grace sitting with Bobbi Jean?

   Ⓐ She doesn't like it.

   Ⓑ She loves it.

   Ⓒ She wants to be Bobbi Jean's friend.

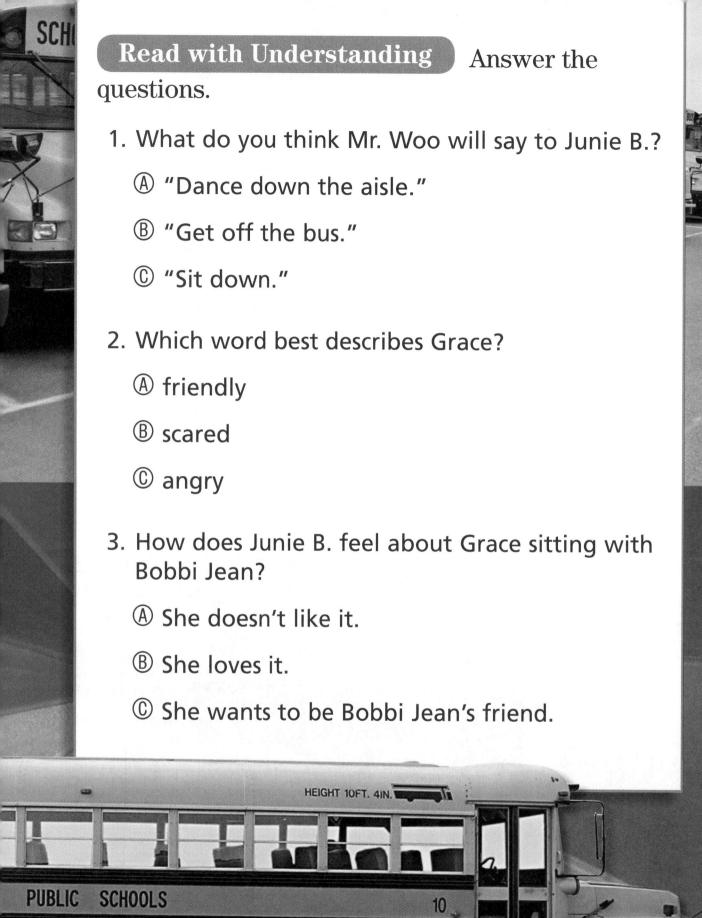

Understand by Seeing It You know what Junie B. is like from what she says and how she acts. On the lines below, write three words that describe Junie B.

Junie B.

_____

_____

_____

Write to Learn   Predict what happens when Junie B. gets to school. Does her bad day get better or worse? Write three sentences describing what you think will happen. Then draw a picture to show what happens.

_____

_____

_____

_____

THE LION and the MOUSE

Listen as your teacher reads. Then answer the questions.

1. Why did the Lion laugh?

    Ⓐ The Mouse thought he could help the Lion.

    Ⓑ The Mouse was tickling his whiskers.

    Ⓒ The Mouse looked funny.

2. Which of the following lessons did the Lion learn?

    Ⓐ Never let a mouse go.

    Ⓑ Don't trust anyone.

    Ⓒ Little friends can be great friends.

Acknowledgments

Reprinted with the permission of Atheneum Books for Young Readers, an imprint of Simon & Schuster Children's Publishing Division, from HENRY AND MUDGE: THE FIRST BOOK by Cynthia Rylant. Text © 1987 Cynthia Rylant.

From ARTHUR TRICKS THE TOOTH FAIRY by Marc Brown, copyright © 1998 by Marc Brown. Used by permission of Random House Children's Books, a division of Random House, Inc.

From JUNIE B., FIRST GRADER (AT LAST!) by Barbara Park illustrated by Denise Brunkus, copyright © 2001 by Barbara Park. Illustrations copyright © 2001 by Denise Brunkus. Used by permission of Random House Children's Books, a division of Random House, Inc.

Historical Fiction

Aesop's Fables

"How-to" Informational

Fiction

"How-to" Info

Folk Rhyme

Indian L

w-to" Informational

ndian Legend

Fa

Short Story

Fiction

Sl

Fiction

Aesop's Fabl

Folk Rhyme

Procedural Information

Historical Fiction

Folk Rh

ble

Aesop's Fables

Narrative Fiction

"How-to" Informational

Aesop's Fables

ural Information

Procedural Infor

ive Fiction

Fable

Fabl

Historical Fiction

Fiction

Short Story

formation

Fable

"How-to" I

zine Article

Procedural Information

"How-to" Informational

Procedural Information